6/4

6966
7866

D0850456

War Music

WAR MUSIC

An Account of
Books 16 to 19
of Homer's *Iliad*

Christopher Logue
Farrar · Straus · Giroux
New York

Copyright © 1981 by Christopher Logue
First published by Jonathan Cape Ltd., 1981
Published by Penguin Books Ltd., 1984
First American printing, 1987
Printed in the United States of America
Library of Congress Cataloging-in-Publication Data
Logue, Christopher.
    War music.
An account of books 16-19 of Homer's Iliad.
1. Achilles (Greek mythology)—Poetry.   2. Patroclus
(Greek mythology)—Poetry.   3. Trojan War—Poetry.
I. Homer. Iliad. Book 16-19. English. II. Title.
PR6023.038W37   1987   821'.914   87-7449

Contents

Introduction

Either the translations of the *Iliad* on which *War Music* is based
did not exist or they had had only a passing interest for me until
1959 when Donald Carne-Ross suggested I contribute to a new
version of the poem he was about to commission for the BBC.

Knowing no Greek I began work on the passage he chose for
me by studying the same passage in the translations published
by Chapman (1611), Pope (1720), Lord Derby (1865), A. T.
Murray (1924), and Rieu (1950).

While Pope was the most and Murray the least accomplished
of these authors, Murray, according to learned gossip, possessed
the most and Pope the least information about Homer's Greek
—though Chapman had tried to abort the charge that his trans-
lation was based on a French crib by calling his judges "envious
Windfuckers"; Lord Derby was high-Victorian- and Rieu mid-
Windsor-steady.

Yet whatever these guides had known about the language in
which the *Iliad* was composed, each of them gave me a quite
dissimilar impression of the work that had inspired their own;
and this variety, plus regular *On Homer* tutorials from Carne-
Ross, supported my plan to retain the storyline of the passage
he had chosen for me, but to cut or to amplify or to add to its
incidents, to vary certain of its similes, and (mostly) to omit
Homer's descriptive epithets, "ten-second-miler-Achilles," "thick-
as-a-pyramid-Ajax," and so forth.

As the work progressed beyond its original limitation I paid
less attention to my guides. Carne-Ross would provide me with
a literal translation that retained the Greek word order; I would
concoct a storyline based on its main incident; and then, know-
ing the gist of what this or that character said, would try to
make their voices come alive and to keep the action on the move.

I was not, then, making a translation in the accepted sense of the word, but what I hoped would turn out to be a poem in English dependent upon whatever, through reading and through conversation, I could guess about a small part of the *Iliad*, a poem whose composition is reckoned to have preceded the beginnings of our own written language by fifteen centuries.

My reading on the subject of translation had produced at least one important opinion: "We must try its effect as an English poem," Boswell reports Johnson as saying, "that is the way to judge of the merit of a translation."

Even though it owes its life to ridicule or to the power of bad taste, any poem that survives outside professional literary circles for more than one generation is noteworthy.

For a poem of over 15,000 lines representing an age as remote from its own as it is from ours to survive the collapse of, not just one society (a serious critical test no poem in English has, as yet, had to pass), but two, could easily mean that those who have kept it alive are mad.

And if it follows that those who read the *Iliad* in translation are merely a bit touched, some of our national problems become clearer: Pope earned the equivalent of £100,000 from his Homer work; my edition of Lord Derby's *Iliad* is its fifth; two million copies of Rieu's version have been sold. In fact, any deficiencies of length or of vigour you may find in what follows may be ascribed to my concern for public health.

War Music comprises Books (as scholars call them) 16 to 19 of the *Iliad*.

My choosing these passages derives from the advice of Carne-Ross. "Book 16, or *Patrocleia*," he said, "might be described as a miniature version of the *Iliad*. It has a quarrel, a making-up, a concession, several battles, the death of a famous leader (Sarpedon), disagreement in Heaven, a human cheeking the Gods, and, as a result of that human's death, an irreversible change.

"In addition to these things, *Patrocleia* contains the *Iliad*'s crucial twist: through the death of Patroclus, Achilles returns to the fight, thereby assuring the destruction of Troy."

Pax, or Book 19, is its opposite: disaffected allies settling their differences in order to avoid defeat at the hands of a mutual enemy. *Pax* lacks fighting; it exemplifies the public confession of common sins righted by material compensation and absolved by formal sacrifice.

With *Pax* completed I realised that conflating Books 17 and 18 as *GBH* (Grievous Bodily Harm, an English legal term for serious forms of criminal assault) would allow me to try my hand at something new—600-odd lines devoted almost entirely to violent, mass action, which, once done, would unite *Patrocleia* and *Pax* into a narrative capable of being read independently of its guessed-at parent.

After *Patrocleia* was first published I started to get critical support not only from those connected with the composition and publication of verse but from those whom we may choose to count among the hopelessly insane: the hard core of Unprofessional Ancient Greek Readers, Homer's lay fans.

Welcome as the support of my like had been, as encouraging, and critically speaking more useful, were my contacts with such fans. "Quite good that bit of Homer you did," one might say. "If you do more of it, have a look at"—citing a favourite passage —"and in case you need any help with the words—take my card."

I took up three such offers. What I learned from those Homerniks clarified the guesses I made about the transmitted text, and my debt to them is considerable.

In addition to Carne-Ross I would like to thank Colin Leach, Peter Levi, Bernard Pomerance, Kathleen Raine, George Rapp, Stephen Spender, and George Steiner for their critical support; and the Bollingen Foundation and the Arts Council of Great Britain for their financial support.

War Music

Prologue

*In the ninth summer of the Trojan War Achilles withdrew his
forces from the Greek Confederacy because Agamemnon ap-
propriated one of his female slaves.*

*Thereafter the Trojans gained the upper hand. Hector raided
the Greek beach-head, crossed the ditch protecting their fleet,
and burned one of its ships. It looked as if the Greeks would be
destroyed.*

*At this moment Patroclus came to Achilles and begged for his
help.*

Patrocleia

Now hear this:
While they fought around the ship from Thessaly,
Patroclus came crying to the Greek.

"Why tears, Patroclus?" Achilles said.
"Why hang about my ankles like a child
Pestering its mother, wanting to be picked up,
Expecting her to stop what she is at, and,
In the end, getting its way through snivels?
    You have bad news from home?
Someone is dead, Patroclus? Your father? Mine?
But news like that is never confidential.
If such was true, you, me, and all the Myrmidons
Would cry together.
    It's the Greeks, Patroclus, isn't it?
You weep because a dozen Greeks lie dead beside their ships.
But did you weep when those same Greeks condoned my wrongs?
If I remember rightly, you said—nothing."

    And Patroclus:
"Save your hate, Achilles. It will keep.
Our cause is sick enough without your grudging it my tears.
    You know Odysseus is wounded?
Orontes, too—his thigh: King Agamemnon, even. Yet
Still you ask: *Why tears?*
    Is there to be no finish to your grudge?
No, no; don't shrug me off. Mind who it is that asks:
Not the smart Ithacan; not Agamemnon. Me.
And God forbid I share the niceness of a man
Who, when his friends go down, sits tight

7

And finds his vindication in their pain.

They are dying, Achilles. Dying like flies.
Think, if you cannot think of them, of those
Who will come after them; what they will say:

Achilles the Resentful—can you hear it?—
Achilles, strong? . . . *The Strongest of the Strong*—
And just as well, because his sense of wrong was heavy.

Shameful that I can talk to you this way."

All still.

"And yet, among the many who do not,
As I believe that God and she who bore
You to a mortal husband back your claim,
So I believe they will not censor mine:

Let me go out and help the Greeks, Achilles.
Let me command your troops. Part of them, then?
And let me wear your armour."

Still.

"Man—it will be enough!
Me, dressed as you, pointing the Myrmidons . . .
The sight alone will make Troy pause, and say:
'It's him,' a second look will check them, turn them,
Give the Greeks a rest (although war has no rest) and turned,
Nothing will stop us till they squat behind their Wall."

And so he begged for death.

"Better to ask yourself," Achilles said,
"If you would stay my friend or not
Than speculate which god, or whether God Himself,
Packaged the specious quibbles with my mouth
Your insolence delivers to my face.

Why not add Agamemnon to your whine?
King vain, king fretful, truthless Agamemnon,
Eager to eat tomorrow's fame today.

Go on . . . *He was a sick man at the time, Achilles.*

He did it to avoid unpleasantness, Achilles.
Achilles, he was not too well advised."
 Staring each other down until he said:
 "O love,
I am so glutted with resentment that I ache.
 Tell me, have I got it wrong?
Did he not take the girl I won?—
And all my fine fair-weather friends agree
That she was mine by right of rape and conquest? Yet,
When it comes to it, they side with him; the royal slug
Who robs the man on whom his crown depends.
 Yet done is done; I cannot grudge forever.
Take what you want: men, armour, cars, the lot."
 Easy to see his loss was on the run;
Him standing, saying:
 "Muster the troops and thrust them, hard,
Just here"—marking the sand—"between the enemy
And the Fleet.
 Aie! . . . they are impudent, these Trojans . . .
They stroke our ships,
Fondle their slim black necks, and split them, yes—
Agamemnon's itchy digits make me absent,
My absence makes them brave, and so, Patroclus,
Dear Agamemnon's grab-all/lose-all flows.
 All right: if not Achilles, then his vicar.
Forget the spear. Take this"—one half its length—"instead.
You say Odysseus is out? Bad. Bad. And Ajax, too?
No wonder all I hear is
Hector, Hector, Hector, everywhere Hector,
As if he were a god split into sixty!
 Hurry, Patroclus, or they will burn us out . . .
But listen first. Hard listening? Good.
 Hear what I want:
My rights, and my apologies. No less.
And that is all.

9

I want the Greeks saved, yes;
Thereafter—Agamemnon at my tent,
With her, Briseis, willing, at my feet;
And many gifts. Be clear about the gifts.
   And one thing more before you go:
Don't overreach yourself, Patroclus.
Without me you are something, but not much.
Let Hector be. He's mine—God willing.
In any case he'd make a meal of you,
And I don't want you killed.
But neither do I want to see you shine
At my expense.
   So mark my word:
No matter how, how much, how often, or how easily you win,
Once you have forced the Trojans back, you stop.
   There is a certain brightness in the air,
Meaning the Lord Apollo is too close
For you to disobey me and be safe.
   You know Apollo loves the Trojans; and you know
That even God our Father hesitates
To contradict Apollo . . .
   O friend,
I would be glad if all the Greeks lay dead
While you and I demolished Troy alone."

Cut to the Fleet.

The air near Ajax was so thick with arrows, that,
As they came, their shanks tickered against each other;
And under them the Trojans swarmed so thick
Ajax outspread his arms, turned his spear flat,
And simply *pushed.* Yet they came clamouring back until
So many Trojans had a go at him

The iron chaps of Ajax' helmet slapped his cheeks
To soft red pulp, and his head reached back and forth
Like a clapper inside a bell made out of sword blades.
    Maybe, even with no breath left,
Big Ajax might have stood it yet; yet
Big and all as he was, Prince Hector meant to burn that ship:
And God was pleased to let him.

    Pulling the Trojans out a yard or two,
He baited Ajax with his throat; and Ajax took.
As the spear lifted, Hector skipped in range;
As Ajax readied, Hector bared his throat again;
And, as Ajax lunged, Prince Hector jived on his right heel
And snicked the haft clean through its neck,
Pruning the bronze nose off—Aie!—it was good to watch
Big Ajax and his spear, both empty topped,
Blundering about for— Oh, a minute went
Before he noticed it had gone.
    But when he noticed it he knew
God stood by Hector's elbow, not by his;
That God was pleased with Hector, not with Ajax;
And, sensibly enough, he fled.

    The ship was burned.

October.
The hungry province grows restive.
The Imperial army must visit the frontier.
Dawn.
The Captains arrive behind standards;
A tiger's face carved on each lance-butt;
And equipment for a long campaign
Is issued to every soldier.

First light.
Men stand behind the level feathers of their breath.
A messenger runs from the pearl-fringed tent.
The Captains form a ring. They read.
The eldest one points north. The others nod.

Likewise his Captains stood around Achilles: listening.
And the Myrmidons began to arm and tramp about the beach.
First sunlight off the sea like thousands of white birds.
Salt haze.

Imagine wolves: an hour ago the pack
Hustled a stag, then tore it into shreds.
And now that they have gorged upon its haunch
They need a drink to wash their curry down.
So, sniffing out a pool, they loll their long,
Thin, sharp-pointed tongues therein; and as they lap
Rose-coloured billows idle off their chops,
Drifting throughout the water like pink smoke.

Likewise his soldiers ready for his eye,
Their five commanders on his right,
Patroclus on his left,
And the onshore wind behind Achilles' voice:

"Excellent killers of men!
Today Patroclus leads; and by tonight,
You, behind him, will clear the Trojans from our ditch.
And who at twilight fails to bring
At least one Trojan head to deck
The palings of our camp, can sleep outside
With Agamemnon's trash."

The columns tightened.
The rim of each man's shield
Overlapped the face of his neighbour's shield

Like clinkered hulls—as shipwrights call them when they lay
Strake over strake, caulked against seas.
　　As they moved off, the columns tightened more;
Until, to one above, it seemed, five wide black straps,
Studded with bolts, were being drawn across the sand.

　　Before Achilles sailed to Troy
His women packed and put aboard his ship
A painted oak box filled with winter clothes;
Rugs for his feet, a fleece-lined windcheater—
You know the sort of thing. And in this box
He kept an eye bowl made from ivory and horn
Which he, and only he, used for Communion.
　　And having spoken to his troops he took it out,
Rubbed sulphur crystals on its inner face,
And washed and dried his hands before,
Spring water rinsed, brimming with altar-wine,
He held it at arm's length, and prayed:

> *"Our Father, Who rules the Heaven,*
> *Because Your will is done where will may be,*
> *Grant me this prayer*
> *As You have granted other prayers of mine:*
> *Give my Patroclus Your victory;*
> *Let him show Hector he can win*
> *Without me at his side;*
> *And grant, above all else, O Lord,*
> *That when the Trojans are defeated, he*
> *Returns to me unharmed."*

God heard his prayer and granted half of it.
Patroclus would rout the Trojans; yes;
But not a word was said about his safe return.

No, my Achilles, God promised nothing of the kind,
As carefully you dried your cup,
As carefully replaced it in its box,
And stood outside your tent and watched
Your men and your Patroclus go by.

Hornets occasionally nest near roads.
In the late spring they breed, feeding their grubs
And feeding off the tacky sweat those grubs exude.
Ignorant children sometimes poke
Sticks into such a nest, and stir. The hornets swarm.
Often a swollen child dies that night.
Sometimes they menace passers-by instead.

No such mistake today.

Swarming up and off the beach
Patroclus swung Achilles' Myrmidons
Left at the ditch.
    Keeping it on their right they streamed
Along the camp's main track; one side, the rampart;
On the other, ships.
    Things were so close you could not see your front;
And from the footplate of his wheels, Patroclus cried:
    "For Achilles!"
As the enemies closed.

The Trojans lay across the ship,
Most of them busy seeing that it burned.
Others slid underneath and were so occupied
Knocking away the chocks that kept it upright,
They did not see Patroclus stoop.
    But those above did.

In less time than it takes to dip and light a match
Achilles' helmet loomed above their cheeks
With Myrmidons splayed out on either side
Like iron wings.
    Dropping the pitch
They reached for javelins, keelspikes, boat-hooks, Oh,
Anything to keep Achilles off—
Have he and Agamemnon patched things up?

    Patroclus aimed his spear where they were thickest.
That is to say, around
The chariot commander, Akafact.
But as Patroclus threw
The ship's mast flamed from stem to peak, and fell
Lengthwise across the incident.
    Its fat waist clubbed the hull's top deck
And the ship flopped sideways.
Those underneath got crunched.
And howling Greeks ran up
To pike the others as they slithered off.
    This fate was not for Akafact:
Because the mast's peak hit the sand no more than six
Feet from Patroclus' car, the horses shied,
Spoiling his cast. Nothing was lost.
    As he fell back, back arched,
God blew the javelin straight; and thus
Mid-air, the cold bronze apex sank
Between his teeth and tongue, parted his brain,
Pressed on, and stapled him against the upturned hull.
His dead jaw gaped. His soul
Crawled off his tongue and vanished into sunlight.

    Often at daybreak a salty moon
Hangs over Ida; and the wind that comes
More than a thousand miles across Asia

Knocks a tile off Priam's roof.
About this time each day for nine long years
His men marched down the Skean road,
Their spears like nettles stirred by wind;
And round about this time each day
The Greek commanders shade their eyes
And squinny through the morning sun;
And since no battle has returned
All of its soldiers, the Trojans wave,
Look back towards the wall, and think
Of those who may require new men next day.

The battle swayed.
Half-naked men hacked slowly at each other
As the Greeks eased back the Trojans.
They stood close;
Closer; thigh in thigh; mask twisted over iron mask
Like kissing.
One moment fifty chariots break out; head for the ditch;
Three cross; the rest wheel back; vanish in ochre dust.
For an instant the Greeks falter. One is killed. And then
The Trojans are eased back a little more;
The ship is cleared, the fire smothered, and who cares
That Hector's chariot opens a new way,
Now moving, pausing now, now moving on again,
And his spear's tip flickers in the smoky light
Like the head of a crested adder over fern?—
Always the Trojans shift towards the ditch.

Of several incidents, consider two:
Panotis' chariot yawed and tipped him
Back off the plate by Little Ajax' feet.
Neither had room to strike; and so the Greek
Knocked his head back with a forearm smash,
And in the space his swaying made, close lopped.

Blood dulled both sides of the leafy blade.
Fate caught Panotis' body; death his head.
    Nearer the ditch Arcadeum met Lycon:
Catching each other's eye both cast, both missed,
Both ran together, and both struck; but
Only Lycon missed both times.
    His neck was cut clean through
Except for a skein of flesh off which
His head hung down like a melon.

    You will have heard about the restless mice
    Called lemmings; how, at no set time, and why,
    No one is sure, they form a grey cascade that pours
    Out of the mountains, down, across the flat,
    Until they rush into the sea and drown.

    Likewise the Trojans as they crossed the ditch.

    From the far bank Hector tried to help them.
Impossible . . .
    He did not guess
So many cars, so many infantry, had crossed;
Engaged, there never seemed enough; but now
They crammed the edge,
The big-eyed horses rearing at the drop,
Their mouths wrenched sideways,
Neck yokes dragged back like saddles.
    And though the drivers looped their reins,
Pegged themselves in, and hauled,
The teetering jam eased forward.
    Only the soft edge held them;
And as the wheels notched into it, the dirt came up
Over the bolts that pinned the axles to the centre-poles,
Horses on one side of the rim,
Cars and men the other.

Stuck.
While other men, infantry,
Meant to be rearguard, climbed into, pulled friends into,
Shouted, struck at who tried to check them, jammed
Spear-poles through spokes—
    Aie . . .
And Patroclus let them, let them,
Let them balance, let them, then cried:
    "For Achilles!"
And drove in.

    As you, Hector, drove off.

So the Trojans nearest to Patroclus squirmed
Away from him towards the ditch; and those
Near falling into it clawed back
Towards Patroclus; and those cram-packed between
Just clawed and squirmed and—
    Why did you leave them, Hector? You
Who had generals like clouds, soldiers like drops of rain,
As you were partway back to Priam's capital
The soft edge gave, and all your glittering soldiery
Toppled into the ditch like swill.

    On certain winter days the land seems grey,
    And the no-headroom left between it and the grey
    Masses of downthrust cloud, fills with wet haze:
    Lines of cold rain weld mile on sightless mile
    Of waste to air: floods occupy the state; and still
    The rains continue, grey on grey;
    God's punishment, say some, on those who bear
    False witness; and some say, on those
    Judges divorced from justice by contempt
    Of those they judge; plus the accomplices of both,
    Perched on their fencing through the vacant day,

Until the water takes them all in all
In one enormous wave into the sea.

The Trojan horses made like this.
As they went up the far side of the ditch
They dragged behind them dead or half-dead charioteers
Who had looped themselves inside their reins.
Better like this, perhaps, than left to Greeks.

Patroclus split the rump.
Some (only a few) followed their horses up
Onto the plain and ran for Troy. The rest
Scurried along the ditch and hid themselves
Among Scamander's fens.

Nothing was left of Hector's raid except
Loose smoke-swaths like blue hair above the dunes,
And Agamemnon's ditch stained crimson where
Some outraged god five miles tall had stamped on glass.

A movement in the air. Gulls lift;
Then sideslip; land again. No more.
Mindless of everything Achilles said
Patroclus went for Troy.

See if you can imagine how it looked:

An opened fan, held flat; its pin
(That marks the ditch) towards yourself; its curve
(That spans the plain) remote:
The left guard points at Troy; the right
Covers the dunes that front the Aegean coast:
Like crabs disturbed by flame the Trojans run
This way and that across its radiants.

Patroclus thrusts his soldiers at the mid
Point of the pleated leaf; a painted sun.

And it was here that Thestor, Enop's boy,
Met that circumstance in nature
Gods call fate, and on this day, men called Patroclus.
    Thestor was not a Trojan.
But when King Priam's satraps came from Troy
And asked Sarpedon, Lycia's Prince, for aid,
And he said, "Yes"—Thestor, the apple of old Enop's eye,
Applied to leave his management and fight
With all his clan. And as he reined away, he called:
    "Do not forsake me, O my seven meadows,
Until I conquer Greece!"
Though all he conquered was six foot of sand.

    Fate's sister, Fortune, favours those
Who keep their nerve.
Thestor was not like this.
He lost his head, first; then his life.
    His chariot bucked too slow over the rutted corpses,
And as Patroclus drew abreast of him,
The terrified boy let the horses baulk,
Leaving the reins to flow beside the car,
And cowered in its varnished basket,
Weeping.
    They passed so close that hub skinned hub.
Ahead, Patroclus braked a shade, and then,
And gracefully as men in oilskins cast
Fake insects over trout, he speared the boy,
And with his hip his pivot, prised Thestor up and out
As easily as later men detach
A sardine from an opened tin.

    Nine more Lycians died on the long run for Troy—
And they were no great trouble.

If a spear missed, Patroclus watched
Their white heels flutter up the plain through dust,
Picked a fresh haft, waited, and pinned his next.

The day seemed done; dust could be left to dust;
Flies had laid eggs in many of the dead;
Until Sarpedon wedged his car across the rout,
Pushed up his mask, and said:

"Well run, my soldiers, but from what?"—
Selecting two light javelins—"Who will wait
To see their known Prince spit
Once and for all this big, anonymous Greek"—
And vaulted off his chariot plate—
"That makes you sweat?"—and flexed himself,
Running his thumb across his points, and scuffed
Dirt toward Patroclus, who climbed down
More slowly; pleased beneath his iron.

It was noon.

God and His wife (who is His sister, too)
Watched them prepare. He, with regret; She,
With satisfaction heard Him out:

"Surely Fate has marked enough good men without Sarpedon?
Shall I return him to his waving plains
Or let . . ."

And She:

"Others beside Yourself have children due today.
If one God saves his bud—why not the rest?

My dear, I know You love Sarpedon; and I know
His death goes hard. Why not do this:
Let him fight bravely for a while; then, when
Patroclus severs him from care and misery,
Sleep and Death shall carry him to Lycia by Taurus,
Remembered by wise men throughout the world
And buried royally."

Noon. Striped mosquitoes. Nothing stirs.

Under the white sun, back and forth
Across a disk of yellow earth, midway
Between the sea and closed stone capital,
The heroes fought like Pharaoh's bare-necked hens
Wrangling over carrion in the air.
They sight each other, stand on their tails,
Lock claws, lie back inside their wings, and hang
High in between the white-faced pyramids,
Each savaging the other's craw.

Likewise the human champions until
Patroclus' spear nosed past Sarpedon's busy heart
And the ground sense in his body leached away.
    Kneeling at first, then laid full length,
Teeth clenched and saying: "Glaucos, be quick
Or they will strip me while I live.
    And if they do it, Glaucos, if
My captured weapons prove their jubilee,
Shame on you, Glaucos, till your dying day.
    So get our best.
Anaxapart, Aeneas, Hector, too—do not miss him-
And cover me with moving blades till sunset.
Then . . ." he was going,
"For my sake, Glaucos . . ." going,
"Kill!"
    And he was gone.
Sunlight reflecting in his dry brown eyes.
    Patroclus in his chariot again,
Wiping his neck, his smiling beard,
About to signal the advance.

    "Listen, Master!"
Glaucos prayed to Lord Apollo,

"Wherever You may be,
And You are everywhere,
And everywhere You hear
Men in their trouble;
Trouble has come to me.
Our best is dead and I
Am wounded, Lord! O Lord
Apollo hear my prayer!
You know me, and You know
That I shall fight until I die,
But I can barely lift my arm!
Lord, put my pain to sleep,
And grant me strength enough to keep
My sword above Sarpedon's corpse
Until the sun obeys Your call to set."

And Apollo, Mousegod, Lord of the Morning, He
Whose face is brighter than a thousand suns,
Mollified his wound with sacred thought,
And let delight in fighting warm his loins.
And He did more: as Glaucos fetched their best,
Apollo called:
    "Sun, stand thou still over Ilium,
And guard Sarpedon's body till their blades
Move over it as grasses over stone."

    Air into azure steel;
The daylight stiffens to translucent horn;
    And through it,
Falling,
    One sun's cord
Opening out into a radiant cone around Sarpedon's corpse;
And him inside that light, as if
A god asleep upon his outstretched hand.

Dust like red mist.
Pain like chalk on slate. Heat like Arctic.
The light withdrawn from Sarpedon's body.
The enemies swirling over it.
Bronze flak.
  Man against man; banner behind raised banner;
The torn gold overwhelming the faded blue;
Blue overcoming gold; both up again; both frayed
By arrows that drift like bees, thicker than autumn rain.
  The left horse falls. The right, prances through blades,
Tearing its belly like a silk balloon.
And the shields inch forward under bowshots.
And under the shields the half-lost soldiers think:
"We fight when the sun rises; when it sets we count the dead.
What has the beauty of Helen to do with us?" Half-lost,
With the ochre mist swirling around their knees,
They shuffle forward, lost, until the shields clash:
—AOI!
  Lines of black ovals eight feet high, clash:
—AOI!
And in the half-light who will be first to hesitate,
Or, wavering, draw back, and Yes! . . . the slow
Wavering begins, and, Yes! . . . they bend away from us,
As spear points flicker in between black hide
Bronze glows vaguely, and bones show
Like pink drumsticks.
  And over it all,
As flies shift up and down a haemorrhage alive with ants,
The captains in their iron masks drift past each other,
Calling, calling, gathering light on their breastplates;
So stained they think that they are friends
And do not turn, do not salute, or else salute their enemies.

But we who are under the shields know
Our enemy marches at the head of the column;
And yet we march!
The voice we obey is the voice of the enemy,
Yet we obey!
And he who is forever talking about enemies
Is himself the enemy!

Light circling the dunes. The flying white.
Larks soar above the soldiers, breathing haze.
And them above, their faces pressed against eternal glass,
The Gods . . .

"The one I fancy," Hera says, "is him."
"The Redhead?"
    "Yes . . ." and whispered over space into his ear:
"King human. Menelaos. If you stick
Him, *him*, and *him*, I promise you will get your Helen back."

See how that Royal fights:
Flaking his blade on Python's hip,
He rakes its splintered edge down Cazca's back,
Tosses aside the stump,
And with his ever-vengeful, empty hands,
Grabs Midon, old King Raphno's eldest son
—Known as Count Suckle to his enemies—
Expert at dicing, good in bed, who once
(Just for a joke, of course) ate thirty vulture's eggs
At one of Helen's parties on the wall.
And later men recalled how he was slain;
One swearing "gutted," one "that he was ripped
Up the front until his belly grinned,"
And some were quite convinced he ran away
And lived ten thousand days beside a cool
And amethystine lake in Phrygia;

But if you want the truth, well . . .
King Menelaos got him by the ears
Bowed back his chubby neck and bit
A lump out of his jugular—
"Sweet God, his dirty blood is in my eyes!
Some Trojan runt will stick me . . ." but
She who admired him wiped the mess away.

If Hector waved,
His wounded and his sick got up to fight;
And if Patroclus called, the Myrmidons
Struck, and called back; with them, as with Patroclus,
To die in battle was like going home.

Try to recall the pause, thock, pause,
Made by axe blades as they pace
Each other through a valuable wood.
Though the work takes place on the far
Side of a valley, and the axe strokes are
Muted by depths of warm, still standing air,
They throb, throb, closely in your ear;
And now and then you catch a phrase
Exchanged between the men who work
More than a mile away, with perfect clarity.

Likewise the sound of spear on spear,
Shield against shield, shield against spear
Around Sarpedon's body.

And all this time God watched His favourite enemies:
Minute Patroclus, like a fleck
Of radium on His right hand,
Should he die now—or push the Trojans back still more?
And on His left, Prince Hector, like a silver mote,
Should he turn coward for an hour
And let Patroclus steal Sarpedon's gear?

The left goes down.
In the half-light Hector's blood turns milky
And he runs for Troy.

It is true that men are clever;
But the least of gods is cleverer than their best.
And it was here, before God's hands
(Moons poised on either side of their earth's agate)
You overreached yourself, Patroclus.
Yes, my darling,
Not only God was out that day but Lord Apollo.
"You know Apollo loves the Trojans: so,
Once you have forced them back, you stop."
Remember it, Patroclus? Or was it years ago
Achilles cautioned you outside his tent?
Remembering or not you stripped Sarpedon's gear,
And went for Troy alone.

And God turned to Apollo, saying:
"Mousegod, take my Sarpedon out of range
And clarify his wounds with mountain water.
Moisten his body with tinctures of white myrrh
And violet iodine; and when these chrysms dry,
Fold him in miniver that never wears
And lints that never fade,
And call my two blind footmen, Sleep and Death,
To carry him to Lycia by Taurus,
Where, playing stone chimes and tambourines,
His tribe will consecrate his death,
Before whose memory the stones shall fade."
And Apollo took Sarpedon out of range
And clarified his wounds with mountain water;
Moistened his body with tinctures of white myrrh
And violet iodine; and when these chrysms dried
He folded him in miniver and lints

That never wear, that never fade,
And called God's two blind footmen, Sleep and Death,
Who carried him
Before whose memory the stones shall fade
To Lycia by Taurus.

Three times Patroclus climbed Troy's wall.
Three times his fingers scraped the parapet.
Three times, and every time he tried it on
The smiling Mousegod flicked him back.
But when he came a fourth, last time,
The smile was gone.
    Instead, from parapet to plain to beach-head, on,
Across the rucked, sunstruck Aegean, the Mousegod's voice,
Loud as ten thousand crying together,
Cried:

"Greek,
Get back where you belong!"

So loud
Even the Yellow Judges giving law
Half-way across the world's circumference paused.

"Get back where you belong!
Troy will fall in God's good time,
But not to you!"

It was Patroclus' turn to run, wide-armed,
Staring into the fight, and desperate to hide
(To blind that voice) to hide
Among the stainless blades.

And as he ran
Apollo dressed as Priam's brother stood
Above the Skean Gate, and strolled
With Hector for a while, and took his arm,
And mentioning the ways of duty, courage, love,
And other perishable joys infecting men,
Dissolved his cowardice with promises.
     Observe the scene:
They stand like relatives; the man, the God,
Chatting together on the parapet
That spans the Gate.
     The elder points. The other nods. And the plumes nod
Over them both. Patroclus cannot see
The uncle's finger leading Hector's eye
Towards his flesh.
Nor can he hear Apollo whispering:
"Achilles' heart will break . . ." And neither man
Thinks that a god discusses mortals with a mortal.

     Patroclus fought like dreaming:
His head thrown back, his mouth—wide as a shrieking mask—
Sucked at the air to nourish his infuriated mind
And seemed to draw the Trojans onto him,
To lock them round his waist, red water, washed against his chest,
To lay their tired necks against his sword like birds.
—Is it a god? Divine? Needing no tenderness?—
Yet instantly they touch, he butts them,
Cuts them back:
—Kill them!
My sweet Patroclus,
—Kill them!
As many as you can,
     For
Coming behind you through the dust you felt
—What was it?—felt creation part, and then

APO

LLO!

Who had been patient with you

Struck.

His hand came from the east,
And in his wrist lay all eternity;
And every atom of his mythic weight
Was poised between his fist and bent left leg.
Your eyes lurched out. Achilles' helmet rang
Far and away beneath the cannon-bones of Trojan horses,
And you were footless . . . staggering . . . amazed . . .
Between the clumps of dying, dying yourself,
Dazed by the brilliance in your eyes,
The noise—like weirs heard far away—
Dabbling your astounded fingers
In the vomit on your chest.

And all the Trojans lay and stared at you;
Propped themselves up and stared at you;
Feeling themselves as blest as you felt cursed.

All of them lay and stared;
And one, a boy called Thackta, cast.
His javelin went through your calves,
Stitching your knees together, and you fell,
Not noticing the pain, and tried to crawl
Towards the Fleet, and—even now—feeling
For Thackta's ankle—ah!—and got it? No . . .
Not a boy's ankle that you got,
But Hector's.

Standing above you,
His bronze mask smiling down into your face,
Putting his spear through . . . ach, and saying:
    "Why tears, Patroclus?
Did you hope to melt Troy down
And make our women fetch the ingots home?
    I can imagine it!
You and your marvellous Achilles;

Him with an upright finger, saying:
    Don't show your face again, Patroclus,
Unless it's red with Hector's blood."
    And Patroclus,
Shaking the voice out of his body, says:
    "Big mouth.
Remember it took three of you to kill me.
A god, a boy, and, last and least, a hero.
    I can hear Death pronounce my name, and yet
Somehow it sounds like *Hector.*
    And as I close my eyes I see Achilles' face
With Death's voice coming out of it."

    Saying these things Patroclus died.
And as his soul went through the sand
Hector withdrew his spear and said:
    "Perhaps."

GBH

And Helen walks beneath a burning tree.
Over her nearest arm her olive stole;
Beneath her see-through shift, her nudity;
A gelded cupidon depletes her woe.

Faultless horizon. Flattish sea.
Wet shore. Wide plain. Look west:
King Menelaos sees Patroclus fall
And thinks: "His death will get us home."
Under a mile away Prince Hector says:
"Thackta, keep watch,"
Who wants Achilles' chariot and pair.
Then climbs into his own. Full lock. And goes.

Before it disappears beneath the sea
The plain due west of Troy accumulates
Into a range of whalebacked, hairy dunes,
Two days' ride long, parallel to the coast,
And, at their greatest, half a bowshot thick:
White, empty beaches, supervised by Greece,
Stretch from the tidemark to their crested cliffs;
But on the landward side, and long before
Their yellows fade through buff into the black
Alluvial plain supporting distant Troy,
Sickle-shaped bays of deep, loose sand, embraced
By corniced horns, appear; and over there

—Much like the foothill of a parent range—
A knoll of osier and grassbound scree,
Known to the enemies as Leto's Chair,
Trespasses on the buff and masks the mouth
Of one such windless bay, in which
Patroclus lies and crouching Thackta dreams:

"I got his love. If I could get his head . . ."

Picture a yacht
Canting at speed
Over ripple-ribbed sand.
    Change its mast to a man,
    Change its boom to a bow,
    Change its sail to a shield:
See Menelaos
Breasting the whalebacks to picket the corpse of Patroclus.
    His face is sad behind his mask; but not sad-soft,
Sad-up-the-hill and contemplate the moon
Until times change.

Thackta, get lost: he has not seen you—yet;
A child beheading parsley grass
Is all you'll be to him, who knows—
If he can get it out—Patroclus' corpse
Will breach Achilles' strike, the Skean Gate,
And Helen's porch; an ample beast, who vaults
The tufted hussock between you and him
And lets his long, grey, bronze-pronged spear,
Sweep, sweep, Patroclus' vacant face, and guards him gone
Raptly as speechless breathers guard their young:
So run!
    But he does not. Prince Hector is his god.

Instead:
    "Get off my meat, Greek king.
I got him first" (a lie) "his flesh is mine."
    Smooth as a dish that listens to the void
The Redhead's face swings up.
    "Dear God," he thinks,
"Who is this lily-wristed titch?"
Picking a blob of dried froth from his lips,
Locking his mud-green eyes on Thackta's blue,
And saying: "Boy,
I can hear your heart.
Who hopes to hold your children on her knee?"

    Hector has found Achilles' sacred pair.
He idles in: "Hi'e . . . hi'e . . . ," his chariot in,
Dapple and grey they are, their reins in sand,
"Hi'e. Hi'e," who move away from him,
No hint of Troy or Thackta in his head.
    Air into lips; speech into Hector's ear.
Apollo's presence, Priam's voice: "My son,"
Who does not hear . . .
    Louder the god. The horses vanish. "Son,
King Menelaos wants Patroclus' corpse.
Thackta has just one spear."

    Whenever Thackta fought he wore
Slung from an oiled tendon round his neck
A cleverly articulated fish;
Each jacinth scale a moving part; each eye, a pearl.
His luck; his glittering christopher; a gift.
    "My name is Thackta, Greek," he said,
And fingered it.
    "Thackta, the son of Raphno, Lord of Tus?"
    "Indeed."
    "And brother of Lord Midon?"

"Yes."

"Here is the news. I killed him earlier today.
Not that his death was worth an ounce of fluff."

Answer him, Thackta; keep him at his chat;
Tell him you like the colour of his horns—
That Helen left a man too old to fuck.
We can see Hector. Hector reads your fix
And will return before this king-sized wart
Upon the body of your world can cast;
So do not cast . . . And yet he does,
And notes—arm up, toe down—the spear approach
King Menelaos' needling mouth, who wills it near,
Observes it streaking through the sunburnt air,
Waits till his face is half its haft's length off,
Then bows—as if to Helen on their wedding day.

And as that often polished leaf slid past,
Offhandedly the bitter Greek reached up
And hooked the tendon around Thackta's neck
And smashed his downwards moving cry against his knee,
And poached his eyes, and smashed and smashed
That baby face, loose as a bag of nuts; and then—
When Thackta's whimpering gained that fine, high shriek,
Dear to a mind inspired by vengefulness—the Greek
Posted his blade between the runny lips,
Increased the number of the dead by one,
Eased his malignant vigour with a sigh,
And scratched; then snapped the thong
And wiggled Thackta's jacinth fish
Between the Heavenly and his royal eye.

No sound. No movement in the bay.
Stripping his victim with professional speed;
Plate-straps between his teeth; Patroclus up—
And—hup!—knees bowed; one last look round;
Now up the whalebacks to the coast.

Not your day, Menelaos, not your day:
Dust in the air? or smoke? a shout—
Source out of sight, but near, but out of sight
Behind the crest, trough, crest, trough, crest;
Now soon, now soon to see
—Put down that armour isolated king—
Hector, with Glaucos and Anaxapart,
Outdistancing the wind that comes from Greece
—"If I leave you, Patroclus, what"—
And Hector's blood-cry, Hector's plume
—"If I do not, what will become of me?"—
Among the other, nodding, orange plumes.
And all their banners rising one by one;
One after one; and then another one
—"Prince Hector's one of them"—
Come between Leto's Chair, the corniced horn,
Fast as a rested python over tile,
Into the yellow bay.
    Bronze tyres. Reflecting breast-straps. You must set
Patroclus' body back upon the sand,
And as the arrows start to splash, back off,
Running towards the backslope, up, a cat
Airborne a moment, one glance back: "Dear God,
Their chariots will slice," splash, "corpse," splash, splash,
"In half," and reach the crest,
And:
    "Ajax!"
And:
    "Odysseus!"
You shout, and run, and run . . .
    And who would not?
    Then Hector's hand goes up.
Up go the horses. Zigzagged sand. Wheels lock.
    And you are off,
As he climbs down.

Eyelight like sun on tin.
   "My Prince?"
Turning Patroclus over with his foot,
   "Yes, Glaucos." Looking up.
No sign of Troy therein.
   "The Greek has gone for help."
   "I know,"
His nostrils fluttering,
   "Give me your axe,"
His mouth like twine.
   "My axe?"
   "You, Manto:
Shell this lookalike and load the armour up."
   Tall plumes go bob.
   "And you—"
(Sarpedon's armourer)
   "Anaxapart"
(Who once had fifty stitches in his face)
   "Up with its shoulders. Yes, like that."
(And you could strike a match upon the scar.)
   "Now stretch its neck across that rock,"
His arm held out behind; still looking down:
   "Glaucos, I asked you for your axe."
Zephyrs disturb their bearskins. Mask meets mask.
Then Glaucos said:
   "Before you use Patroclus' fat to grease
Your chariot hubs, Overlord Hector, ask yourself how
Troy can be held without Sarpedon's men.

   Dog in the forehead but at heart a deer,
Recall the luckless morning when you kicked
Your silk-and-silver counterpane aside
And found your coast alive with shrieking Greeks.

   After the shock of it, was not Sarpedon's name
The first to cross your lips? whose help you begged?
Though all you brought was 'We would be obliged'

And '*Thankyou, thankyou*' when he promised it—
Keeping his promise with half Lycia.
    And on the day we came,
Before Aeneas and yourself had stopped
Mow multiplying thanks by previous thanks
Sarpedon and Anaxapart had armed,
Gotten our troops together and engaged.
    That day, and every long successive fighting day,
He was first out, last home; with laughter,
Golden wounds, good words; always the first,
First across Agamemnon's ditch today.
    But now that he is dead and has no fellow,
How do you keep your obligation, Hector?
    Begging my axe to violate the one
Greek corpse sufficiently revered to change for his;
Wanting Achilles' gear to pod your beef;
And giving Helen's reject time to fetch
More of our enemies up.
    I know ... I know ..."
Ingathering his reins:
    "Day one, a friend; day two, a guest; day three, a chore.
Sarpedon's death makes me the Lycian chief.
Why should we risk ourselves for Hector's Wall
Who leaves his ally naked in a ditch?"

    Thin
Wavering heat. Big flakes of sand. Live things
Blown right and left.
    The tail-end of a banner wraps
A soldier's face: "Why fight?
The wind brings leaves enough to light a fire."

    "You will not die saluting, Glaucos—will you?"
Prince Hector said. And to the rest:

4   3

"Get the bones home. When Greece comes back
I shall be good enough to watch."

Patroclus naked now.
The armour stacked beneath a chariot rug.
Manto beside the horses, eyes cast down,
Awaiting Hector's word.

"Lead on."

Silent as men grown old while following sheep
They watch him wheel away.

Sea-bird's eye view:
Soldiers around Patroclus: centaur ants
Hoisting a morsel,
    And,
On the whalebacks' tidal side,
Ajax and Little Ajax, Helen's man,
Odysseus and his driver, Bombax, head
A wedge of plate-faced Greeks.
    Close-up on Bombax; 45; fighting since 2;
Who wears his plate beneath his skin; one who has killed
More talking bipeds than Troy's wall has bricks;
Whose hair is long, is oiled, is white, is sprung,
Plaited with silver wire, twice plaited—strong?—
Why, he could swing a city to and fro with it
And get no crick; whose eye can fix
A spider's web yoking a tent peg to its guy
Five miles downbeach—and count its spokes:
    "By night?"
See them come padding down the coastal lane,
Flow up the low-browed, crested cliffs, across the backs;

Two hundred plus; then, at Odysseus' sign, drop flat,
And steer their helmets through the sabre grass,
Lining the shoulders of the bay to look
Down upon Glaucos and the corpse.
　"Ready?" Odysseus says.
Their massed plumes nod.

　Moving at speed, but absolutely still,
The arrow in the air. Death in a man
As something first perceived by accident.
　Massed hands; massed glare;
The piston-kneed, blade-flailing Greeks pour down,
Like a gigantic fan with razored vanes,
Leaping the hummock-studded slope, up-down,
As if the ground between each clump was taut,
Was trampoline, up-down, so slow they fly,
So quick upon the sand.
　Glaucos an instant blinded by the sky
White backflash off their polished front; but in the next,
Scanning them through its after-image, cool
As the atrium of a mossy shrine, and shouts:
　"Close! Close!"
Too late, alas. Before his voice is out
Their masks are on him like a waterfall!
　Who was it said
That one long day's more work will see it done?
Up to the waist in dead:
　"*Dear Lord,*" he prays,
　"*Dear Lord,*" his soldiers dead,
　"*By day,*"
Their souls like babies rising from their lips,
　"A *river in the sky,*"
"Keep close!"

"By night, an Amazon.
Save us from this and I will build a stone"
"Close! Closer still!"
"Temple that bears"
"Now slope your shields!"
"Shadows of deer at sunset and Thy name."
Clenching his men about Patroclus' corpse;
Faced by a fly; all eyes; an egg with eyes;
"We have it still!"—attacked by eyes—"Edge out . . ."
Arrows that thock, that enter eyes, that pass
Close as a layer of paint, that blind,
That splash about them like spring rain.
Bombax takes heads
Like chopping twelve-inch logs for exercise;
Feathers of blood surround him like a bronze
On decorative water; "Hector, where?—
Dog in the forehead but at heart a doe,"
As sunlight jumps from cheek to shiny cheek,
Eager to glorify their transience.
"Not to climb Leto's Chair. That way lies death,
Anaxapart," who does not hear, his eyes
On Pyrop, *The Macedonian Ham*
(As Little Ajax christened him)
The richest and the fattest Greek
(A chariot factory plus numerous farms)
To sail from Liminaria to Troy;
Who looks behind him, half crouched down,
As timid and as fearful as a dog
About to shit.
"Run, Greek—run, run,"
Anaxapart insists. And (fool!) instead
Of burrowing among the shields, he does,
And running cries:
"My mother is alone, and old, and sick,"
But what fear urged obesity held back.

Six arrows in the Lycian's fist:
   "My"—one,
   "Is"—two,
   "And"—three,
   Then—four, —five, —six
In the air at once . . . Wi'eeee!
Even Odysseus paused to catch that trick.
—And the arrows go so fast their shanks ignite!
—And the hits make Pyrop flounce!
—And he cannot hold his mud!
Six hammer blows upon his neck; and long before his voice,
So high, so piteous and profound, died out,
Anaxapart's keen zanies sheared his tin.
   Pleasure maybe
But not a sign of victory in this.
   Glaucos shows red:
Bent as if seen through water, split tip hooked,
Both edges blunted on Greek flesh, his sword.
   "This is our end, my Lord,"
His feet go backwards, treading on the dead
That sigh and ooze like moss.
   "Heaven is silent;
   Earth does not confide;
   I turn around,
   The way to Troy is barred."
Patroclus in their midst. Around him, shields.
Around the shields, the masks.
   "Close! Close!"

Achilles' armour was not made on earth.
A lame god yoked its spacious particles.
Deliberate inattention has
Only enhanced its light-collecting planes;

Into whose depth, safe, safe, amid the dunes
Prince Hector looks, amazed, and strips his own;
Stands naked in the light, amazed, and lifts
Its bodice up, and kisses it; then holds it out,
And, like a man long kept from water, lets
Its radiance pour down; and sees within
The clouds that pass, the gulls that stall,
His own hope-governed face, and near its rim,
Distorted as the brilliant surface bends
Its rivetless, near-minus weight away,
His patient horses, and his men.

    Then,
Through the azure vacancy in which
Our cooling onion floats: clouds long as lips,
God's lips above the mountain, saying:
    "Worm:
Your death is nearer than your nose.
'*Perhaps*,' you told Patroclus as he went.
Perhaps was wrong. But I will let you fight
Dressed as the gods are dressed,
And give your heart a priceless boost, until
Oblivion's resistless whisper bids
Its pulse, a drum between two torches in the night,
To follow your creation on their way."

    The clouds have altered now:
Upgathered like a continental shelf
Crowned by mauve air, and down their pillowed range
Emerald-stained chrome through leaf to orange-grey,
Clear to the listening eye their caves read dusk:
Though that dim porch is Ganges' length away.

    Hector is in the armour. Boran lifts
A coiling oxhorn to his lips. And though

Its summons bumps the tower where Priam sits
Beside a lip that slides
Out of a stone lion's mouth into a pool,
The king is old and deaf, and does not move.

One thousand Trojan soldiers form a ring.
They link their arms; they breathe in unison;
Lay back their faces till each throat stands wide,
And wait; and wait; then, on the masterbeat,
Shatter the empyrean with a cry!
Then stamp! Then cry! Then stamp again! Then cry!
Cry overfollowing cry, concordant stamp
On stamp, until the far, translucent hue
Augments their promising to die, and rides
Forward to sunset on their "God for Troy!"
Hector is in the middle of that ring;
Crouched on his toes; his knees braced wide; palms up;
White dactyls tigered; arms outspread.
And now his certain, triple-armoured mind
(By God, the holy metal, and his men)
Grows light, grows lucent, clarified for death.
And as their voices mix above their prince,
He rocks from toe to toe; and as they stamp,
First one and then the other of his feet
Lifts from the sand; and as they lean and lead
Into a skip-step sunwise traipse around,
Though Hector keeps his body jack-knifed down,
Adding his voice to theirs he starts to turn
Counter their turn, to lift himself, to spin,
Becoming in their eyes a source, a sun,
A star, whose force is theirs, who leaps—
Unfolds his body in the air,
Prances upon the air, and in the air

Unsheaths Achilles' sword and makes it sing . . .
　　See how they flow towards him, arms upraised,
Table their shields to keep his dance aloft,
And cry again, and cry, and start to pour
Over the dunes, him spinning on that top,
Across the buff and onward to the bay,
Achilles' blade about his waist, so fast,
A cymbal struck by voices, shimmer struck,
Out of whose metal centre Hector's own,
Seething between his teeth, wails up the sky
On one insatiable note.
　　And as his wail spread outward on the air,
And as the stolen armour ate the light,
Those fighting round Patroclus' body thought
Earth had upthrust a floe of luminous malt
That swamped their world and pitched the famous Greeks
Back to the crest and filled the bay with waves.
　　And surfacing upon that molten sludge
With Glaucos in his arms, Prince Hector said,
As he wiped the crawling stains away:
　　"Remember me?"
Aeneas going by so close
His slipstream pats their cheeks,
　　"Remember me?"
And rings Patroclus with a horse-high,
Set-too-close-for-the-point-of-a-spear's-tip
Wall of a hundred oxhide shields.

　　Impacted battle; dust above a herd.
Trachea, source of tears, sliced clean.
Deckle-edged wounds: "Poor Jataphact, to know," knocked clean
Out of his armour like a half-set jelly,
"Your eyes to be still open yet not see," or see

By an abandoned chariot a dog
With something like your forearm in its mouth;
A face split off,
Sent skimming lidlike through the crunch,
Still smiling, but its pupils dots on dice:
   Bodies so intermixed
The tremor of their impact keeps the dead
Upright within the mass. Half-dragged, half-borne,
Killed five times over, Caphno—rose with his oar,
Sang as his rapt ship ran its sunside strake
Through the lace of an oncoming wave—now splashed
With blood plus slaver from his chest to chin,
Borne back into the mass, itself borne back
And forth across the bay like cherry froth.
   Someone breaks out; another follows him;
Throws, hits, rides on; the first—transfixed—
Hauls on the carefully selected pole
Trembling within his groin, and drags
His bladder out with it;
Then doubles popeyed back into the jam.
   Notice the Cretans, Little A. & Big—some team!
Prince Little loves to tease them with his arse:
   "I'll screw your widow, Badedas,"
Shouting head down, his face between his knees;
And when the angered Trojan throws, *he* throws,
Twisting and catching what the other threw,
And has the time to watch his leaf divide
His fellow soldier from the light and goes
"No third green generation from his tree,"
Whistling away.
   The Greeks swear by their dead. The Trojans by their home.
"Not one step back—" "If I should die—" and does.
Water through water: who can tell whose red, whose roar
It is? Their banners overclouding one by one;
One after one; and then another one.

5 1

Anaxapart has tied Patroclus' body to a shield:
Spreadeagled on its front,
With Zeeteez and Opknocktophon as crucifers.
And, much as their posterity will spurn
Vampires with garlic, ignorance with thought,
Those Trojans elevate his corpse and claim:
  "Gangway for Troy!"
While in the chariot length their idol gains,
With fingerbells and feathered necklaces,
Molo the Dancer from Cymatriax tugs
At its penis as he squeaks:
  "Achilles' love!"
  Trumpets behind the corpse; more Trojan masks;
Then tambourines and drums: "Not one step back . . ."
But must! "Troy!" "Troy!" "If I—" and does.

  Seeking a quiet eddy in the flood;
Blood flowing from his nostrils; he who fights
Without the aid of anger says: "Antilochos.
Run to the Fleet. Give Wondersulk our news.
His love is dead. His armour gone.
Prince Hector has the corpse.
And as an afterthought, that we are lost."
  "Why me, Odysseus?"
  "That is the why. Now go,
And not so gloomy, if you wish to please."
  Fast as the strongest wing can fly
Between the twilight and the setting sun,
He goes.

  Big Ajax is not one for thought.
Monkeys and rats avoid his company.
Now he is lost. He looks about. He stands
As one who listens for a far-off call,
And now and then, refocussed, knocks

An optimistic blade aside,
Or reaches out and grabs what passes by.
And all the while his huge, packed heart,
Trying to squeeze an answer from its brain:
"Lord, we will crack. I know it. We will crack,"
Until young Manto, Hector's ward,
Came to the stymied giant's aid.

    "Stay here. We do not cut green wheat,"
Prince Hector ordered as he led the dance.
Five minutes later Hector's word became
"I am at least a mile away" from where
Arrows like raindrops slash through boiling dust;
Then walked; then dropped; then: "Only ten lengths more"
—Though on your hands and knees it still seems far—
And saw—head up—dead Caphno's chariot and pair
Come wandering down the outskirt of that day:
"My prize! My prize!"—on, up, flick, off—"My prince,
You will be proud of me!"—away . . .
    But once upon the plate the battle's roar
—Wind larruped flame through stands of dry garrigue—
Inspired his disobedience, swamped his car;
And how the fights blur by, and how the wind
Snaffles the yellow tatter of his hair:
"Did Hector lie? There is no danger here.
And who is that Greek beast, breathless and faint,
Leaning upon his spear, so out of time
That I can run him down?" O downy sprat,
That crocodile is Ajax.
And though his mind is worlds away his eye
Has registered your blip long since,
Signalled his back to bend, his fingers to select
A stone, young Manto, bigger than your head,
Rowed back his elbow, thrown it true, and, true,
It did not, was not aimed at you, that hit

The left horse—splat!—between its gentle eyes,
Dead on the hoof and dragged its tracemate down,
And forwarding your body through the air,
Your please-Prince-Hector-help-me open mouth
Swallowed the nose of Ajax' canted spear.

Harder than painting snowfields in full sunlight
The light in Ajax' eye, his answer come:
    Out with your sword; up, aim, and in-
To the living horse with it. The traces cut.
Then feel the shaft rise freely to your hand.
    And like a man who thrusts a glowing rake
Into an opened furnace, Ajax picked
Dandiprat Manto off his spear,
Then rammed dead Caphno's chariot through the Greek-
Cum-Trojan flux.
    And now the Greeks are speaking with one voice:
"Patroclus ours!" across the dark they call,
And echoing this counted chicken, Troy:
"Who gets the body shares the gold with me!"
And all: "Are these my arms,
So tired they go on, and on, alone?"

Elsewhere late afternoon goes lazily enough.
No sign of cloud. Small noises cross the air intact.
    And yawning as he leaves his tent
To sigh and settle back against a rope—
As some men settle into life
Quiet in quiet rooms, supplied
With all they need by mute, obedient hands—
Achilles: who does his best to blimp
The queasy premonitions that explode beneath his heart:

"No matter how, how much, how often, or how easily you win—
O my Patroclus, are you bitten off?"

Antilochos appearing through these words.
Hateful the voice that springs between his clear-edged lips,
Weakening Odysseus' message to: "Is gone."

Down on your knees, Achilles. Farther down.
Now forward on your hands and put your face into the dirt,
And scrub it to and fro.
 Grief has you by the hair with one
And with the forceps of its other hand
Uses your mouth to trowel the dogshit up;
Watches you lift your arms to Heaven; and then
Pounces and screws your nose into the filth.
 Gods have plucked drawstrings from your head,
And from the template of your upper lip
Modelled their bows.
 Not now. Not since
Your grieving reaches out and pistol-whips
That envied face, until
Frightened to bear your black, backbreaking agony alone,
You sank, throat back, thrown back, your voice
Thrown out across the sea to reach your Source.

Salt-water woman,
Eternal,
 She heard him;
Long-bodied Thetis who lives in the wave,
 In the coral,
 Fluorescent;
Green over grey over olive forever;

The light falling sideways from Heaven,
She heard him,
   Achilles,
Her marvellous son.

   Surge in her body;
Head ferns grow wider,
   Grow paler;
Her message, his message,
   Goes through the water:
   "Sisters,"
Nayruesay,
   "Sisters,"
Eternal,
   Salt-water women,
Came when she called to them,
Came through the waves to her, swam as she swam
Towards Greece; beyond Greece; now she passes the Islands,
Arm over arm swimming backways, peaked nipples,
Full fifty green-grey palely shimmering kith of King Nayruce,
Those who leave eddies, who startle, her sisters:
   Derna, Leucate, lithe Famagusta,
Isso, Nifaria, black chevroned Cos,
Panope, beaded, entwining Galethiel,
Thasos, Talita, Hymno and Phyle,
Sleek Manapharium, Jithis, Bardia,
Serpentine Xanthe, Nemix and Simi,
Came from the iodine, surfaced through azure
Onto the beach-head and lay round Achilles.

   "What cause have you to weep?" his mother said.
"It was your hands God saw, your voice He heard
Uplifted, saying: 'Lord, until they feel my lack,
Let the Greeks burn; let them taste pain.' "
   And heard him say:

5 6

"Poor Source—
Wet-cheeked, much-wronged, long-suffering Thetis,
Famous in time as the Eternal Moan,
That dowry of Heaven-sent weapons you brought
My brutal father when your father forced
You to divide your legs for oafish him,
Pods Hector now; and I, the paradigm
Of all creation's violent hierarchy,
Sit naked by the sea and number waves.
    Excellent that my Greekish aides taste pain;
And better that they die. But not enough.
Not agony enough. Increase that pain;
Without appeal and without delay
Let death come down—and not, please God
(For I will be His master either way),
Exclusively to Agamemnon's led;
But onto Troy; and onto Troy Beyond; and unto all of us
Brain-damaged, stinking herd of God-foxed sheep,
Chiefs of our loathsome, thought-polluted dot—
Bar two: Hector's dark head is mine."

    "You cannot have it without armour, child,"
His mother said.
And vanished through the waves with all her school.

    Sunfade. Sea breathing. Sea-lice trot
Over warm stones.
    Achilles and Antilochos:
How small they look beneath the disappearing sky!
    Sap rises in them both. An opening breeze
Ruffles their hair; but only A. hears:

    "Greek . . ."
    "Yes?"
    "Greek . . ."
    "Who?"

"Iris."

"Speak."

"Go to the ditch.
Let Troy know you are back.
Until your strength is operational
Your voice must serve.
    You know what fighting is:
When things are at their worst an extra shout
Can save the day."

He goes.

Consider planes at touchdown—how they poise;
Or palms beneath a numbered hurricane;
Or birds wheeled sideways over windswept heights;
Or burly salmon challenging a weir;
Right-angled, dreamy fliers, as they ride
The instep of a dying wave, or trace
Diagonals on snowslopes:

Quick cuts like these may give
Some definition to the mind's wild eye
That follow-spots Achilles' sacred pair—
No death, no dung, no loyalty to man
In them—come Troyside down the dunes towards the bay,
Achilles' charioteer, Alastor, lost
On their basket's plate, locked to their reins,
Pulling with all his might to make them stay,
That also Iris heard, that know their Care,
Their semi-human Clay, their half-loved, half-obeyed,
Half-childlike lord, Achilles, will demand

Their services: each worth at least
An income of ten thousand men a day.

At night at Priam's table Hector sits
Beside Aeneas. So it is now.
Square into Greece their two-edged axe heads go,
Sledgehammers on detested statuary,
The bar from which all Trojan wires are drawn.

Head-lock, body-slam,
Hector attacking;
    His anger, his armour, his:
"*Now, now, or never, O Infinite, Endless Apollo,*"
    But silent,
    "*I, in my weakness, beseech you to cast
All thought of peace on earth for me away
Without possession of that corpse.*"
    Hard to say who is who: the soldiers, the captains,
Their guts look alike.

Ajax alone between it and their thirst:
Pivoting on his toes, his arms looped up,
Safe in his hands his spear's moist butt, that whirrs
—Who falls into that airscrew, kiss goodbye . . .
And for a moment Hector driven back,
And when, and if, and here it comes:
"On! On! On! On!" he cries. "Die on that spear!"
The Trojans try to snake beneath its point,
And Ajax down on one, and with the other foot
Thrusts himself round until the spear's bronze torque
Hisses a finger's width above Patroclus' face,

As Bombax shouts: "Here, Ajax, here,"
As Menelaos: "Here . . ."

And while his brother keeps his back, Aeneas taunts:
"Crapulous mammoth! Thicker than the wall!
Ajax the wordless chattel of his strength!"—
And spits, and runs, and, yes, the Greek is hooked!
Who follows him, and throws . . . A hit?
Odysseus holds his breath: "Alas—Apollo hates that shot":
Forth went the hand of clarity across the twilit air
And tipped the straight-grained, bronze-fanged pole aside.

"God scum," said Bombax—only to himself.

Aeneas through the blades, brushing their strokes aside,
Up the far slope, with Ajax far behind,
And sees Alastor entering the bay
Between the horn and Leto's Chair,
And sprints towards its brink,
And . . . two, one, off!—
    Free fall—
    Free fall—
Swooping upon Alastor in his car,
As angels in commemorative stone
Still swoop on unknown soldiers as they die
For some at best but half-remembered cause.
    And as Alastor swerved, Aeneas' axe
Enhanced the natural crackage of his skull,
And he quit being, while his pair
Skid-slithered through the tumult, flailed that mass,
And overran Patroclus' tattered corpse.
    Hector triumphant:
Dropping his spear, clenching his fists,
Raising his fists in the air, shaking his fists with delight:
    "Who brings it out will share the fame with me!"

Anaxapart has got it by the chin.
Knees bent, spine bowed, feet braced into the clavicles,
Wrenching the nut right left right right, thinks:
"Screw the bastard off . . ."
Leaning across Anaxapart Prince Hector shouts, "On! On!"
Trying to slash at Bombax and the Greeks,
Who have Patroclus by the feet, and tug:
    "Ah . . ."
They tug.
    "Ah . . ."
The body stretched between them like a hide.

Five miles due north.
Achilles on the rampart by the ditch:
    He lifts his face to ninety; draws his breath;
And from the bottom of his heart emits
So long and loud and terrible a scream,
The icy scabs at either end of earth
Winced in their sleep; and in the heads that fought
It seemed as if, and through his voice alone,
The whole world's woe could be abandoned to the sky.

    And in that instant all the fighting glassed.

    Odysseus excepted.

    Quick as a priest who waits for passing birds
To form a letter in the air, he has
Patroclus' body up and out.
    And as Prince Hector shouts:
"The Greeks have got their carrion intact!"
    The sun,
Head of a still-surviving kingdom, drew

The earth between them and himself,
   And so the plain grew dark.

   Starred sky. Calm sky.
Only the water's luminosity
Marks the land's end.

   A light is moving down the beach.
It wavers. Comes towards the fleet.
The hulls like upturned glasses made of jet.

   Is it a God?
No details

   Yet.

   Now we can hear a drum.

   And now we see it:
Six warriors with flaming wands,
Eight veteran bearers, and one prince,
Patroclus, dead, crossed axes on his chest,
Upon a bier.

   Gold on the wrists that bear the prince aloft.
Tears on the cheeks of those who lead with wands.
Multiple injuries adorn the corpse.
And we, the army, genuflect in line.

   Five years ago Achilles robbed a Phrygian citadel
And kept the temple cauldron for himself.

The poet who accompanied him to Troy
Deciphered the inscriptions on its waist.
One said:
I AM THE EARTH
The other:
VOID.

And when from zigzagged ewers his female slaves
Had filled and built a fire beneath its knees,
Achilles laved the flesh and pinned the wounds
And dressed the yellow hair and spread
Ointments from Thetis' cave on every mark
Of what Patroclus was, and kissed its mouth,
And wet its face with tears, and kissed and kissed again,
And said: "My love, I swear you will not burn
Till Hector's severed head is in my lap."

Pax

Rat.
Pearl.
Onion.
Honey:
These colours came before the Sun
   Lifted above the ocean,
Bringing light
   Alike to mortals and Immortals.

And through this falling brightness,
Through the by now:
   Mosque,
   Eucalyptus,
   Utter blue,
Came Thetis,
Gliding across the azimuth,
With armour the colour of moonlight laid on her forearms;
Her palms upturned;
Her hovering above the fleet;
Her skyish face towards her son,

   Achilles,
Gripping the body of Patroclus
Naked and dead against his own,
While Thetis spoke:
   "Son . . ."
His soldiers looking on;
Looking away from it; remembering their own;
   "Grieving will not amend what Heaven has done.

Suppose you throw your hate after Patroclus' soul.
Who besides Troy will gain?
    See what I've brought . . ."

    And as she laid the moonlit armour on the sand
It chimed;
    And the sound that came from it
Followed the light that came from it,
Like sighing,
Saying,
    Made in Heaven.

    And those who had the neck to watch Achilles weep
Could not look now.
    Nobody looked. They were afraid.

    Except Achilles: looked,
Lifted a piece of it between his hands;
Turned it; tested the weight of it; and then
Spun the holy tungsten, like a star between his knees,
Slitting his eyes against the flare, some said,
But others thought the hatred shuttered by his lids
Made him protect the metal.

    His eyes like furnace doors ajar.

    When he had got its weight
And let its industry console his grief a bit:
    "I'll fight,"
He said. Simple as that. "I'll fight."

    And so Troy fell.

    "But while I fight, what will become of this"—
Patroclus—"Mother?

Inside an hour a thousand slimy things will burrow.
And if the fight drags on his flesh will swarm
Like water boiling."
    And she:
"Son, while you fight,
Nothing shall taint him;
Sun will not touch him,
Nor the slimy things."

    Promising this she slid
Rare ichors in the seven born openings of Patroclus' head,
Making the carrion radiant.
    And her Achilles went to make amends,
Walking alone beside the broken lace that hung
Over the sea's green fist.

The sea that is always counting.

Ever since men began in time, time and
Time again they met in parliaments,
Where, in due turn, letting the next man speak,
With mouthfuls of soft air they tried to stop
Themselves from ravening their talking throats;
Hoping enunciated airs would fall
With verisimilitude in different minds,
And bring some concord to those minds; soft air
Between the hatred dying animals
Monotonously bear towards themselves;
Only soft air to underwrite the in-
Built violence of being, to meld it to
Something more civil, rarer than true forgiveness.
No work was lovelier in history;
And nothing failed so often: knowing this
The army came to hear Achilles say:
"Pax, Agamemnon." And Agamemnon's: "Pax."

Now I must ask you to forget reality,
To be a momentary bird above those men
And watch their filings gather round
The rumour of a conference until
Magnetic grapevines bind them close.
    From a low angle the army looks oval, whitish centered,
Split at one end, prised slightly open, and,
Opposite to the opening, Achilles
(Who they have come to hear) with hard-faced veterans
On either side, lance-butts struck down,
And here and there a flag. Even the chariot mechanics,
Tentmakers, priests, and whores came up
To hear their Lords say pax.

And as men will, they came, the limping kings;
Odysseus first, chatting to Little Ajax, through the ring,
Sitting them down; and after them, a trifle slow
But coming all the same, doomed Agamemnon,
King of Kings, his elbow gummed with blood.

    The ring is shut. Enormous calm.
King Agamemnon and Achilles face to face,
Distinct as polygon and square.

    Achilles first:
"King,
I have been a fool.
The arid bliss self-righteousness provokes
Addled my mind."
    Odysseus nods.
"Remembering how I took Briseis' town,
And how its women offered me their flesh—
Like simple creatures looking for a passage to the sea—
It would have been far better for us both
If, when the winnings were aligned,

I had ignored her urgent vulnerability.
But, having made it so, I like my own.
And if another man—my King, what's more—
Takes what is mine and lets the army know it,
What are they both to do?
 Kings can admit so little.
Kings know: what damages their principality
Endangers all.
 If he is inconsiderate,
He is the king; if greedy, greedy king,
And if at noon the king says: '*It is night*.'—
Behold, the stars!
 What if he damages the man
On whom his principality depends?
He's still the king. His war goes on. The man must give.
 But if the man in question cannot give
Because the god in him that makes the king his chief dependant
Is part and parcel of the god that cries *Revenge!* when he is wronged,
What happens then?
 Stamp on my foot, my heart is stunned;
I cannot help it; it is stunned; it rankles—
Here," touching his chest.
 "I am not angry anymore.
My heart is broken. Done is done, it says.
And yet its pain can only mask my rancour.
So let pride serve.
When all is said and done—I am Achilles."

 And the army love their darling, and they cry:
"Achil! Achil! Achil!"
Louder than any counting sea;
And sentries on the eastern wall of Troy
Sweat by their spears.

 King Agamemnon waits.

And waits.

Then rising, says:

"Heroes . . .
I do not think your zeal will be injured
If those who are the farthest off stand still,
And those in front stop muttering to themselves."
   Bad start.
"Everyone can't hear everything, of course."
   Gulls cry.
"However, even clear-voiced heralds,
Accustomed as they are to public speaking,
Can lose their audience if inattention makes them feel
Indifference to their message."
   Gulls.

"In fact, the things I have to say, are, in a sense,
Meant for Achilles' ears alone.
But if the army and his peers witness our settlement
My purpose will be better served.
   Like him, I am a man.
But I am also king. His king. Your king.
And as your king I have received
What most of you have not unwillingly agreed was mine:
The best part of the blame."
   He has them now.
"BUT I AM NOT TO BLAME!"
   And now.
"Undoubtedly I took, unfairly, pulling rank,
The girl Achilles won.
I tell you it was not my wish.
Between my judgement and my action Ahtay fell;
God's eldest girl, contentious Ahtay . . . Oh,

Soft are her footsteps but her performance keeps no day;
Nor does she walk upon the ground, but drifts
Into our human wishes like the sticky flecks of down
Tickling our lips in endless summertime;
And with her episode comes misery.
   Let me remind you how God walked
Into the courtyard of the Sun and told his cabinet:
   'Rejoice with me!
   For unto men this day a child is born
   Whose blood is royal with my eminence;
   And who, all in good time, will be
   A king called *Hercules*.'
And looking at her fingers, Hera said:
   'We have been fooled before.
   However; if you swear
   That any child of yours born on this day . . .'
God swore; and Ahtay sat between His eyes.
Soon as the oath had crossed His mythic lips
Hera went quick as that from Heaven to Greece,
And with her right hand masked the womb
Swaddling Hercules, and with her left
Parted the body of another girl whose child was His
But only eight months gone,
And held it up and jeered:
   'See what your oath has done!'
   God made the early boy a king, and Hercules a serf
And wept as men must weep.
   If you will lead the Greeks, Achilles,
I will give Briseis back;
   And may we be forgiven."

The sun is smaller now.

Achilles says: "Let us fight now—*at once*—"

"Wait"—slipping the word in like a bolt—
"Marvellous boy," Odysseus says.
    "You can do what you like with us except make men fight hungry.
    Well . . . you could do that too, but . . ."
Turning away from him towards the ranks—
    "Wait!
The king will keep his promise now.
Young lords will fetch his penal gifts
For everyone to see and be amazed.
    Everyone knows that men who get
Angry without good reason will
Conciliate without free gifts.
    Therefore Achilles gladly takes
Everything Agamemnon gives.
    And he who gives steps free of blame,
As he adopts the wrong.
God bless them both."

Then, squatting by Achilles, says:
"Boy—you are the best of us. Your strength is fabulous.
But in my way I know some things you don't.
In any case, I'm old. Let me play wise.
    What we have got to do is not embroidery.
For you, the battle may be gold.
The men will enter it like needles,
Breaking or broken, but either way,
Emerging naked as they went.
    Think of the moment when they see
The usual loot is missing from this fight
Although the usual risks are not.
They do not own the swords with which they fight;
Nor the ships that brought them here;
Orders are handed down to them in words
They barely understand; frankly,
They do not give a whit who fucks soft Helen.

Ithaca's mine; Pythia yours; but what are they defending?
They love you? Yes. They do. They also loved Patroclus;
And he is dead, they say; bury the dead, they say;
A hundred of us singing angels died for every knock
Patroclus took—so why the fuss?—that's war, they say,
Who came to eat in Troy and not to prove how much
Dear friends are missed.
    Certainly, they are fools.
But they are right. Fools often are.
    Bury the dead, Achil,
And I will help you pitch Troy in the sea."

    Cobalt in Heaven,
And below it
    Polar blue.
The body of the air is lapis, and
    Where it falls
Behind the soft horizon,
The light turns back to Heaven.

    A soldier pisses by his chariot;
Another
    Sweetens his axe blade on a soapy stone;
And up between the dunes,
With ribbons, tambourines, and little drums,
Come twelve white horses led by seven women,
Briseis in their midst,
Her breasts so lovely that they envy one another.
    And they pass by . . .
And after them young lords, escorting
Twenty ewers of bright silver, each in a polished trivet,
Their shining cheeks engraved by silversmiths
With files of long-nosed soldiers on the march.

And they pass by . . .
And after them, a sledge
Piled with twelve lots of Asian gold,
Carefully weighed, worth a small city.
    And they pass by . . .
And last of all, guarding a sacrificial hog,
Talthibios, Chief Herald of the Greeks,
Passed by into the centre of the ring.

    Yellow mists over Mount Ida.
The hog lowers its gilded tusks.
Is still.

    By Agamemnon's feet, Talthibios sprinkles barley;
Snips a tuft from the hog's nape;
Waits for a breeze to nudge it off his palm
Into the flames that burn between the army and its king.

    Haze covers Mount Ida.
Sand falls down sand.
Even the Gods are listless.

    And Agamemnon spreads his arms,
Raises his face towards the sun, and cries:

    "GOD
Be my witness;
EARTH
My witness;
SUN, SKY, WATER, WIND,
My witness.
I have not tampered with the girl
I took unjustly from Achilles."

And drags his knife across the hog's silk throat.

Mists over Ida.

Slaves gut and throw the dead hog in the sea.

The army like ten thousand yellow stones.

    Achilles says:
"So be it.
Eat, and prepare to fight."

    And took Briseis to his ship.

    Under the curve the keel makes
Where it sweeps upright to the painted beak,
Achilles' tetrarchs placed their gilded oars,
Set twelve carved thwarts across them, then
Surfaced this stage with wolf- and beaver-fleece;
Amid whose stirring nap Patroclus lay:
The damaged statue of a prince awaiting transportation.
    Near it Achilles sat, Odysseus beside,
And women brought them food.
    "Patroclus liked to eat," Achilles said,
"And you cooked well, Patroclus, didn't you?
Particularly well that summer when
The royal cuckold, crown in hand, came visiting from Argos
Whining 'wife' and 'theft' and 'war' and 'please' and—
What is this *eat*, Odysseus?
If you were telling me: He's dead, your father; well . . .
I might eat a bit; troubled, it's true; but eat
Like any fool who came God knows how many mist-
And danger-mixed sea-miles to salvage Helen.
    Oh, I know you, Odysseus. You think:
Achilles will fight better if he feeds.

Don't be so sure.
    I do not care about his gifts. I do not care, Odysseus,
Do not care!
    Patroclus was my life's sole love.
The only living thing that called
Love out of me.
At night I used to dream of how, when he came home to Greece,
He'd tell them of my death—for I must die—and show my son
This house, for instance; or that stone beside the stream;
My long green meadows stretching through the light
So clear it seems to magnify . . ."

    And here Achilles falls asleep beside his dead;
Odysseus goes off, as close to tears
As he will ever be;
    And,
At a window of the closed stone capital,
Helen wipes the sweat from under her big breasts.
    Aoi! . . . she is beautiful.

But there is something foul about her, too.

Now I shall ask you to imagine how
Men under discipline of death prepare for war.
There is much more to it than armament,
And kicks from those who could not catch an hour's sleep,
Waking the ones who dozed like rows of spoons;
Or those with everything to lose, the kings,
Asleep like pistols in red velvet.
Moments like these absolve the needs dividing men.
Whatever caught and brought and kept them here,
Under Troy's ochre wall for ten burnt years,
Is lost: and for a while they join a terrible equality;
Are virtuous, self-sacrificing, free;
And so insidious is this liberty

That those surviving it will bear
An even greater servitude to its root:
Believing they were whole, while they were brave;
That they were rich, because their loot was great;
That war was meaningful, because they lost their friends.
They rise!—the Greeks with smiling iron mouths.
They are like Nature; like a mass of flame;
Great lengths of water struck by changing winds;
A forest of innumerable trees;
Boundless sand; snowfall across broad steppes at dusk.
As a huge beast stands and turns around itself,
The well-fed, glittering army, stands and turns.

Nothing can happen till Achilles wakes.

He wakes.

Those who have slept with sorrow in their hearts
Know all too well how short but sweet
The instant of their coming-to can be:
The heart is strong, as if it never sorrowed;
The mind's dear clarity intact; and then,
The vast, unhappy stone from yesterday
Rolls down these vital units to the bottom of oneself.

Achilles saw his armour in that instant,
And its ominous radiance flooded his heart.
   Bright pads with toggles crossed behind the knees,
Bodice of fitted tungsten, pliable straps;
His shield as round and rich as moons in spring;
His sword's haft parked between sheaves of grey obsidian,
From which a lucid blade stood out, leaf-shaped, adorned
With running spirals.
   And for his head a welded cortex; yes,
Though it is noon, the helmet screams against the light;

Scratches the eye; so violent it can be seen
Across three thousand years.

Achilles stands; he stretches; turns on his heel;
Punches the sunlight, bends, then—jumps! . . .
And lets the world turn fractionally beneath his feet.

Noon. In the foothills
Melons emerge from their green hidings.
Heat.

He walks towards the chariot.
Greece waits.

Over the wells in Troy mosquitoes hover.

Beside the chariot.
Leading the sacred horses; watching his driver cinch,
Shake out the reins, and lay them on the rail;
Dapple and white the horses are; perfect they are;
Sneezing to clear their cool black muzzles.

He mounts.

The chariot's basket dips. The whip
Fires in between the horses' ears;
And as in dreams, or at Cape Kennedy, they rise,
Slowly it seems, their chests like royals, yet
Behind them in a double plume the sand curls up,
Is barely dented by their flying hooves,
And wheels that barely touch the world,
And the wind slams shut behind them.

"Fast as you are," Achilles says,
"When twilight makes the armistice,

Take care you don't leave me behind
As you left my Patroclus."

   And as it ran the white horse turned its tall face back
And said:
   "Prince,
This time we will, this time we can, but this time cannot last.
And when we leave you, not for dead—but dead—
God will not call us negligent as you have done."

   And Achilles, shaken, says:
"I know I will not make old bones."

   And laid his scourge against their racing flanks.

Someone has left a spear stuck in the sand.

Guide to Pronunciation

Cymatriax	Cy·mat·tri·ax
Ida	Ey·der
Ithaca	Ith·tha·ka
Liminaria	Lim·in·ah·ree·ah
Lycia	Ly·see·ah
Phrygia	Phri·gee·ah
Pythia	Pi·thee·ah
Scamander	Ska·man·der
Skean	Skee·an
Taurus	Taor·us
Thessaly	Thess·a·ly

MORTALS AND IMMORTALS

Aeneas	Ae·nee·as
Ahtay	Ah·tay
Akafact	Ak·a·fact
Alastor	Al·ass·tor
Anaxapart	An·ax·a·part
Antilochos	An·til·o·kos
Arcadeum	Ar·kay·de·um
Badedas	Bad·day·das
Bardia	Bar·dee·ah
Bombax	Bom·bax
Boran	Bore·an
Briseis	Bri·see·is
Caphno	Caph·no
Cazca	Caz·ca
Cos	Coss
Derna	Der·na

Enop	Ee·nop
Famagusta	Fa·ma·gus·ta
Galethiel	Gal·ee·thiel
Glaucos	Glau·cos
Hera	Hear·a
Hymno	Him·no
Isso	Iss·o
Jataphact	Ja·ta·phact
Jithis	Gee·this
Leto	Lee·toh
Leucate	Leu·ka·tay
Lycon	Ly·con
Manapharium	Ma·na·pha·ree·um
Manto	Man·toh
Menelaos	Men·na·lay·us
Midon	My·don
Molo	Mow·lo
Myrmidons	Myr·mi·dons
Nayruce	Nay·ruce
Nayruesay	Nay·rue·say
Nemix	Ne·mix
Nifaria	Ni·far·ia
Opknocktophon	Op·knock·toh·phon
Orontes	O·ron·tes
Panope	Pan·oh·pe
Panotis	Pan·oh·tis
Patroclus	Pa·trock·lus
Phyle	Phy·lee
Priam	Pry·am
Pyrop	Py·rop
Raphno	Raph·no
Sarpedon	Sar·pee·don
Simi	See·me
Talita	Tal·lee·ta
Talthibios	Tal·thy·bios

Thackta	**Thack**·ta
Thasos	**Thas**·sos
Thestor	**Thess**·tor
Thetis	**Theet**·is
Xanthe	**Xan**·thee
Zeeteez	Zee·teez

SHOUTS

Aie	Eye·eeee
Aoi	**A**·oy